AF800795

The Bytes Family On Computer Basics

Volume No. 1

ISBN 978-0-615-73916-8
90000
9 780615 739168

Author , Angela Williams-Nash
Illustrations and photos by AnRice Nash

Acknowledgement

No part of this publication may be reproduced in completely or in part, or stored in a retrieval system or transmitted in any form or by any means, electronic, mechanical, photocopying, recording, or otherwise, without the written permission of the author. For information regarding permission email: thebytes@comcast.net.

ISBN: **978-0-615-73916-8**

Copyright

Published by A Nash & Associates. Contact the author by e-mail at ***thebytes@comcast.net*** and visit her blog at ***http://nashontechnology.blogspot.com***.

Printed in the United States of America

The Bytes Family On Computer Basics

TABLE OF CONTENTS

Chapter 1. Introduction

Hello, my name is Rom and I am 10 years old. I live in Computown, USA with my Dad, Mom, big sister Ram, and pet bug Bit. We are the Bytes Family.

People use computers everyday at home, school, and work. I wrote this book to help kids like you learn more about computers and how they work. This is a big job so I asked my family to help. We will work together to share what we know with you. Here is how it will work. At the beginning of every chapter, Mom will provide a list of vocabulary words and a list of key words. ***Vocabulary*** words are in bold like the word **storage**. Understanding the **definition** makes reading more enjoyable. ***Keywords*** are in bold and yellow highlight like the word **computer**. Look for definition of keywords as you read. These words are the main idea, what you should learn from reading.

Ram and I will keep you company as you read the assignment. Remember to go back to the vocabulary list if you do not remember the definition of a word in bold. At the end of this book, my pet bug Bit will list the most important things you should know. This page can be used as a study sheet.

My Dad always says *practice makes perfect*. Practice exercises are at the end of the book. Dad will review the directions before you start each activity. Email me at **thebytes@comcast.net** to let me know what you think!

I hope you are ready like me so let's get started.

Chapter 2. Vocabulary and Keywords Lists

Hello boys and girls, I am Queen Bytes. My son Rom asked me to go over the vocabulary words and keywords. ***Vocabulary*** words with **definitions** are in the purple text box. The definition or meaning of each word is on the next page. ***Keywords*** are in the green text box. You will learn more about keywords as you read.

Vocabulary Words

definition (n) - the meaning of a word

device (n) - a piece of equipment that has a special use

directions (v) - to show or tell how to do something

electronic (n) - a device that uses electricity

logical (adj) - done in way that makes sense

operation (n) - the act of following steps in order to find the answer

perform (v) - to act or to do

record (n) - something that recalls or tells about past events

several (adj) - more than two but not very many

storage (n) - a place or space for storing; memory

Chapter 3. What is a Computer?

Hi, I'm Ram. My brother Rom and I use **computers** every day. We use them to read, do homework, and play games. In the box below, write three things you use a computer do to. When you are done, share your list with a friend or family member.

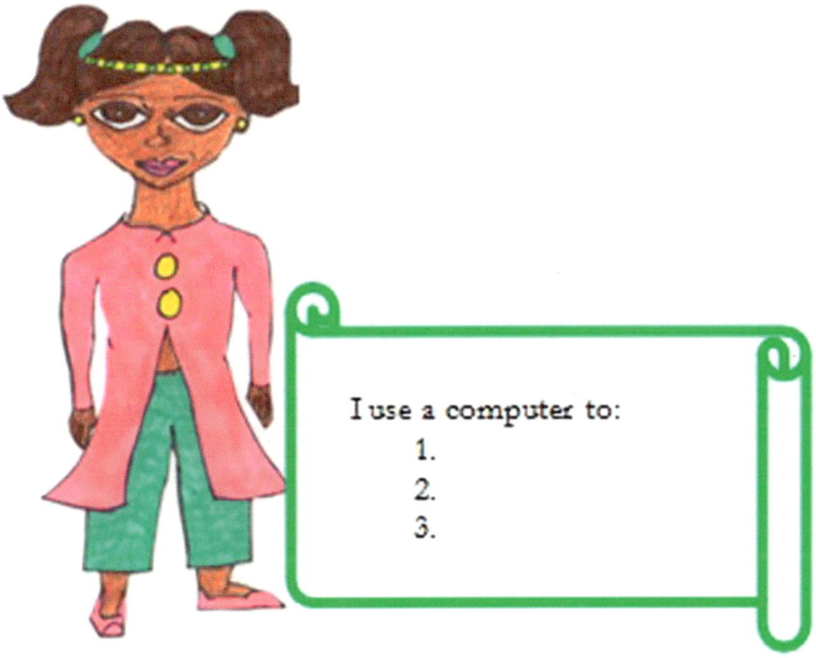

Although many people see and use computers daily, most cannot give a good **definition** of what a computer is. So, we will begin with a good definition of a computer. A **computer** is an **electronic device** that accepts data, stores data, processes data, and output results. A computer system has all the parts needed to make your computer work!

Chapter 4. Parts of a Computer System

Hi everyone, it's Rom again! In this chapter, I will talk more about data and the different parts of a computer system. Computers need data. **Data** is things like words, sounds, music, pictures, and numbers that you want to save for later use.

The chart next to me shows the devices all computers need to work. All computer systems must have an input device, storage device, processor, and output device. Let's learn more about the parts of a computer system!

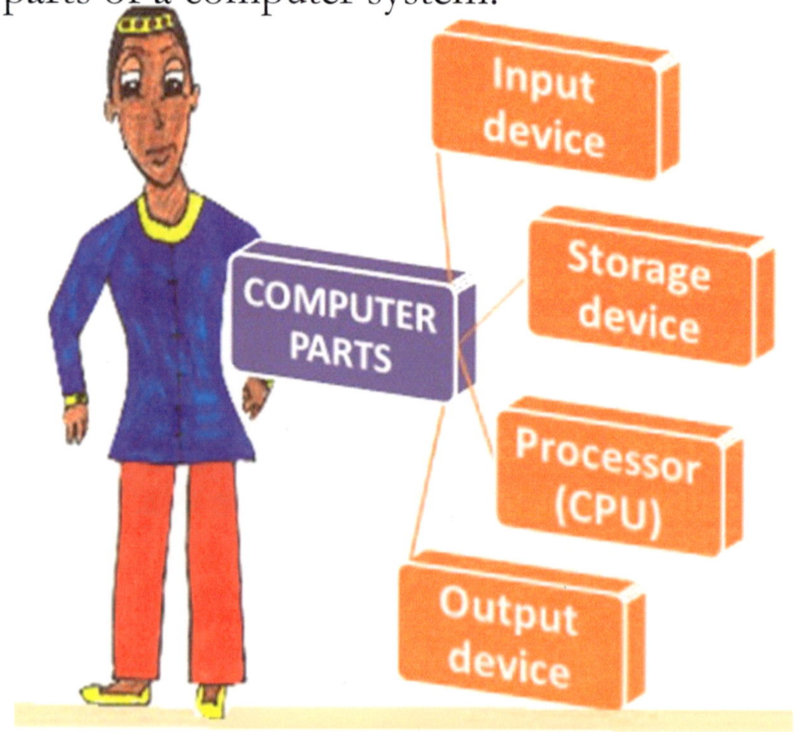

Input devices allow you to put data into the computer. Common input devices include the keyboard, mouse, and microphone. Look at the pictures below.

Keyboard

Mouse

Microphone

Keyboards are used for typing. The **mouse** is used to move around the computer screen and give instructions. **Microphones** are used to **record** sounds.

Once you put data into your computer, it has to go somewhere. The **storage device** that handles data is called a **hard drive**. It holds data for later use. This device also handles the reading and writing of data. Here is a picture of a hard drive.

After you input data and store it, you will want to use it. The **Central Processing Unit (CPU)** that is called a **processor** is the part of a computer that **performs logical** and mathematical **operations** on data. Your computer may have a processors inside.

As you input, store, and process data, you are going to want to see your results. **Output devices** allow you to see, hear, and print data. Common output devices include the computer screen, printer, headphones, and speakers. These devices are shown below.

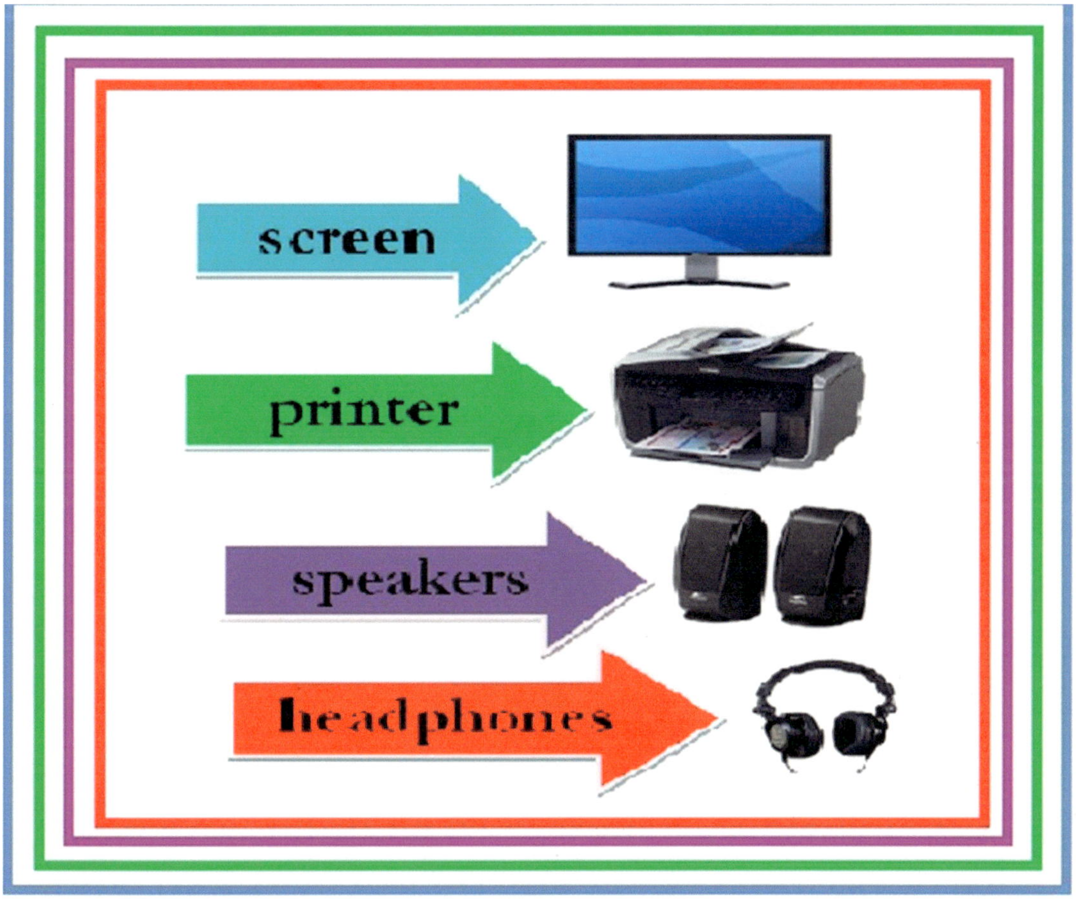

The **screen** is used to see what you have typed into your computer. The **printer** will copy what is on your screen onto a piece of paper. The paper that comes out of a printer is called a **hardcopy**. **Speakers** and **headphones** are used to hear sounds like words and music.

Chapter 4. Recap With Bit

Hi, I'm Bit! It's nice to meet you! Here is a list of what you should know after reading this book.

1. A **computer** is an **electronic device** that accepts data, stores data, processes data, and output results.
2. **Data** is things like words, sounds, music, pictures, and numbers that you put into and store in your computer.
3. All computer systems must have an input device, storage device, processor, and output device to work.
    a. **Input devices** like the keyboard, mouse, and microphone put data into the computer.
    b. **Storage devices** like a hard drive hold data for later use.
    c. The CPU or **processor** performs logical and mathematical operations on data.
    d. **Output devices** like the screen, printer, headphones, and speakers allow you to see, print, and hear stored data.
4. **Hardcopy** is the paper from the printer.

Chapter 5. Practice Exercises With King Bytes

Hello boys and girls! I am King Bytes. Now that you finished reading this book on Computer Basics, it is time to do some activities.

Completing activities is a fun way to learn. I always tell me kids that *Practice makes perfect!* There are five short activities in this section:

1. Word search puzzle,
2. Vocabulary sheet,
3. Keyword sheet,
4. Picture match puzzle, and
5. Critical thinking question

Have fun with these activities. Make sure you read the directions before starting each activity. If you are stuck, go back into the text and find the answer or ask a friend or grownup for help. Compare and discuss your answers with a friend. When you are done, check your answers against the solution at the end of the book.

Activity No. 1 - Computer Basics
Word Search Puzzle

Directions: Read the words in the table below. Find the word in the puzzle.

```
s m e y l v z q d a v w x a t o l h n k
l t o n p a w w a r f j r p m u o h f e
o n o u o i c y t i a e j l r t b m j u
e w f r s h l i a u c m n i o p t w s e
o n d j a e p t g i d l j o f u v k p n
p k p h r g o o n o i t c u r t s n i o
e i u e x v e o r w l s p i e d i x v i
r p i a n p r d z c i x n o p e z d j t
a q o j z t r h e c i p g b x v q b r i
t b n v c i a o l v u m q s d i y o x n
i a c e t r r s c t i e i t t c u q p i
o c l i d p k v d e w c w z b e m m c f
n e c c k e q e x a s x e v u g w d i e
o i o u c p v i n a r s x r f k i y a d
j p j i k i g f p d r a o b y e k p j e
y y v a c r e c o r d v u r j e g y u p
d e c e i i m w r j c u y x u e m c z s
d e r m n u p r k v t v n h h n s c y q
e i r l b b n u h a r d d r i v e n j v
u c g n p b m x o f a j l d z q c a c f
```

data	definition	device
electronic	hardcopy	hard drive
input device	instruction	keyboard
logical	microphone	mouse
operation	output device	perform
processor	record	storage device

Activity No.2 Vocabulary Review

Directions: Use the vocabulary table below to fill in the correct answer. There is only one correct answer. Share your sentences with another person.

definition	logical	perform	storage	instruction
electronic	several	record	operation	device

1. The ______________________ is the meaning of a word.
2. More than two but not very many is ________________.
3. Use ____________________ when you want something done in way that makes sense.
4. To act is to ____________________.
5. Another word for memory is ___________________.
6. A device that uses electricity is ______________________.
7. A ___________________ recalls or tells about past events.
8. _______________________ is a set of directions to follow.
9. The act of following steps in order is called a ______________.
10. A ___________ is a piece of equipment that has a special use.

Activity No. 3 Keywords Review

Directions: Use the keywords table below to fill in the correct answer. There is only one correct answer. Share your sentences with another person.

computer	data	hard drive
input device	keyboard	microphone
output device	processor	screen

1. Words, sounds, music, pictures, and numbers are examples of computer (a)____________.
2. An (b)____________ ________ is used to put data like pictures and music into a computer.
3. The (c)____________ performs logical and mathematical operations in a computer.
4. An electronic device that accepts data, stores data, processes data, and output results is called a (d)____________.
5. Storage device that is built into your computer is called a (e)______ ______.
6. Headphones and printers are examples (f)____________ ________.
7. The (g)____________ and (h)____________ are examples of input devices.
8. The (i)____________ is an example of an output device.

Activity No. 4 Picture Match Puzzle

Directions: Match the word to the picture. Draw a line from the word to the picture.

microphone
processor
printer
headphone
screen
speakers
keyboard
mouse
hard drive

Activity No. 5 Critical Thinking Question

Directions: Students use computers for many different things. On a separate piece of paper list three things you use a computer to do. Make sure you give examples.

Activity Solutions

Activity No. 1 Solution

S	M	E	+	L	+	+	+	D	+	+	+	+	+	+	O	+	+	+	+
+	T	O	N	+	A	+	+	A	+	+	+	+	+	M	U	+	+	+	+
+	+	O	U	O	+	C	+	T	+	+	+	+	+	R	T	+	+	+	+
+	+	+	R	S	H	+	I	A	+	C	+	+	+	O	P	+	+	+	+
O	+	+	+	A	E	P	+	G	I	+	+	+	+	F	U	+	+	+	N
P	+	+	+	+	G	+	O	N	O	I	T	C	U	R	T	S	N	I	O
E	+	+	+	+	+	E	O	R	+	L	+	+	I	E	D	+	+	+	I
R	+	+	+	+	P	R	D	+	C	+	+	N	+	P	E	+	+	+	T
A	+	+	+	+	T	R	H	E	+	I	P	+	+	+	V	+	+	+	I
T	+	+	+	C	+	A	O	+	V	U	M	+	+	+	I	+	+	+	N
I	+	+	E	+	R	+	+	C	T	I	+	+	+	+	C	+	+	+	I
O	+	L	+	D	+	+	+	D	E	+	C	+	+	+	E	+	+	+	F
N	E	+	C	+	E	+	E	+	+	S	+	E	+	+	+	+	+	+	E
+	+	O	+	C	+	V	+	+	+	+	S	+	+	+	+	+	+	+	D
+	P	+	I	+	I	+	+	+	D	R	A	O	B	Y	E	K	+	+	+
Y	+	V	+	C	R	E	C	O	R	D	+	+	R	+	+	+	+	+	+
+	E	+	E	+	+	+	+	+	+	+	+	+	+	+	+	+	+	+	+
D	+	+	+	+	+	+	+	+	+	+	+	+	+	+	+	+	+	+	+
+	+	+	+	+	+	+	+	H	A	R	D	D	R	I	V	E	+	+	+
+	+	+	+	+	+	+	+	+	+	+	+	+	+	+	+	+	+	+	+

Activity No.2 Solution

storage	logical	perform	definition	instruction
electronic	several	record	operation	device

1. A definition is the meaning of a word.
2. More than two but not very many is several.
3. Use logical when you want something done in way that makes sense.
4. To act is to perform.
5. Another word for memory is storage.
6. An electronic device that uses electricity.
7. A record recalls or tells about past events.
8. instruction is a set of directions to follow.
9. The act of following steps in order operation.
10. A device is a piece of equipment that has a special use.

Activity No. 3 Solution

computer	data	hard drive
input device	keyboard	microphone
output device	processor	screen

1. *(a)* data

2. *(b)* input device

3. *(c)* processor

4. *(d) computer*

5. *(e)* hard drive

6. *(f) output devices*

7. *(g)* keyboard *(h) microphone*

8. *(i) screen*

Activity No. 4 Solution

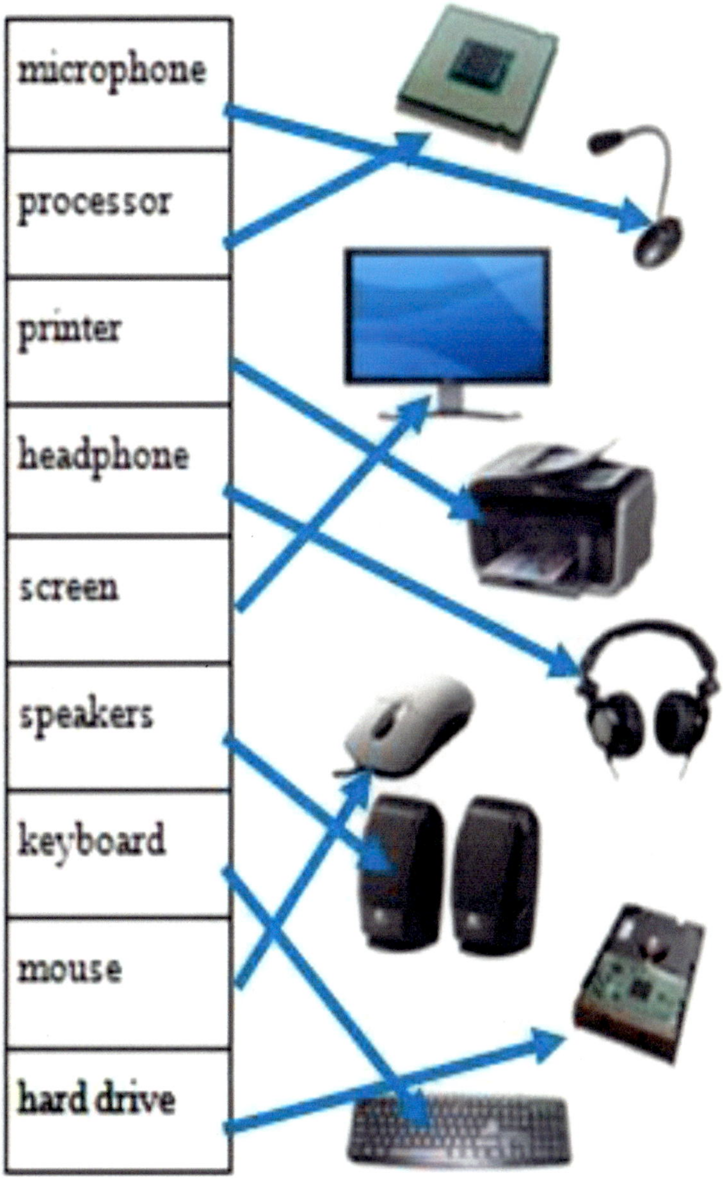

Made in the USA
Monee, IL
05 November 2026

67378012R00017